THE
BLUFFER'S GUIDE
TO
SKIING

DAVID ALLSOP

D0957879

Oval Books

Published by Oval Books
335 Kennington Road
London SE11 4QE

Telephone: (0) 20 7582 7123
Fax: (0) 20 7582 1022
E-mail: info@ovalbooks.com

First published by Ravette Publishing, 1992
First published by Oval Books, 1999

Reprinted 2000

Series Editor – Anne Tauté

Cover designer – Jim Wire, Quantum
Printer – Cox & Wyman Ltd
Producer – Oval Projects Ltd

The Bluffer's Guides® series is based
on an original idea by Peter Wolfe.

The Bluffer's Guide®, The Bluffer's
Guides®, Bluffer's®, and Bluff Your
Way® are Registered Trademarks.

Cover:
The author's pre-war wooden skis and
bamboo poles – vital accoutrements for
bluffing, but less so for skiing.

ISBN: 1-902825-62-4

CONTENTS

INTRODUCTION

Skiing requires a commitment to pleasure of the sort endorsed by hedonists, layabouts, ne'er do wells and philanderers – in other words, a single-minded approach to absolute self-indulgence.

Skiers are deeply flawed people*, so it will come as no surprise to learn that most of them are also extremely proficient bluffers. All skiers will remember that triumphant moment when they first skied down to a crowded restaurant terrace without falling over. Flushed with pride they will have stopped and puffed up their chests in the fond belief that onlookers were bursting with admiration for them. In fact onlookers were doing nothing of the sort, waiting patiently instead for someone else to fall over so that they could point at them and jeer.

But in that brief moment of triumph, the discerning tyro will have discovered a profound truth about skiing. All skiers, irrespective of their age, sex or ability, like to pretend that they are better skiers than they actually are. That axiom lies at the root of the sport, and from that root flourishes the most luxuriant verbiage of preposterous declarations about imagined skills and expertise.

This book will give you a few easy-to-learn hints and techniques which will allow you to be accepted as a skier of rare ability and experience. But it will do more. It will give you the key to the ultimate bluff: how to impress legions of marvelling listeners with your knowledge and advice – without anybody discovering that you can't ski to save your life.

* What else can one call the dangerously obsessed?

HOW IT ALL STARTED

The British have always claimed to have invented Alpine skiing, a remarkable feat bearing in mind the paucity of Alps in the British Isles. But let's not split hairs. Alpine skiing, for those who hadn't really thought about it, is that particular discipline of the sport which involves skiing downhill. It is the most popular variety of the three main forms of skiing. Skiing along on a level gradient is generally known by those who find it tedious as 'poling', or by those who find it interesting as 'langlauf' (invented and, unaccountably, hugely enjoyed by Norwegians). It is also known, more commonly, as 'cross-country' skiing. Uphill skiing is known either as 'ski-touring' or, more commonly, 'absolutely bloody exhausting'.

The British did, in fact, invent Alpine skiing – but were not the first to spot the potential of binding wooden planks to their feet as a means of transportation. That responsibility lies with the Swedes, or possibly the Finns, or possibly the Laps, or the Norwegians, or maybe even the Russians. The Mongols and Turks are also keen to state their own case for having invented it. So too are the Chinese. Sinologists will happily produce ancient manuscripts which mention 'mu-ma' – literally men on 'wooden horses' travelling at the speed of a galloping thoroughbred across the Manchurian plains. This suggests that even during the Tang dynasty primitive skiers on primitive equipment could have happily seen off the British Olympic downhill team.

The oldest 'ski' in existence was found in a peat bog in Hoting, Sweden, and dates from 2,500 BC. Some cave drawings showing hunters on skis dating from about the same time have been found in Rodoy, Norway. But it wasn't until the 1820s that skiing came into its own as a sport when the Norwegians started cavorting about in the snow on skis. They loved it. By the middle of the century they were holding organised cross-country races for 'gentlemen'. But in a competition in Oslo in 1868 a farm hand called Sondre Norheim turned up and spoiled everyone's fun by winning every race. The secret of his success was a ski he had designed himself, with a 'waist' and a secure binding.

Sondre sank without trace from whence he came, but his invention found its way to the Great Exhibition in Paris 20 years later. One interested purchaser was a doctor from Switzerland who took the new skis back to Davos, put them in his attic and then forgot about them. A few years later they were discovered by his apprentice called Branger, and it was he and his brother who became known as the Davos 'Plank-Hoppers'.

Nobody took them too seriously until Sir Arthur Conan Doyle turned up one day in 1894 and asked to be shown how to plank-hop. The lads took him over the mountain pass to Arosa and Sir Arthur was smitten. Writing prophetically in *Strand Magazine* a short while later, he observed: 'I am convinced that the day will come when hundreds of Englishmen will come to Switzerland for the 'ski'-ing season.'

Sure enough Henry Lunn, inventor of the modern package holiday, arrived in the early 1900s with his newly founded 'Public Schools Alpine Sports Club' and promptly colonised the Swiss Alps with carefully selected members of the British upper classes. The bemused Swiss claimed that they needed a passport to get into their own towns and villages.

The British then set about training their diligent and industrious hosts to get them to the top of mountains with the minimum of fuss. They demanded that trains be installed, or else. This is where the Swiss came into their own because, as everyone knows, they like trains a lot. Within a few years there was barely a skiable mountain left in the Alps which didn't have a train going up it, or round it, or through it. Once at the top, the British would get out, put on their skis and hare off to the bottom, making as much noise as possible. Previously, the whole point of skiing had been to get from one point to another – and nobody could quite see the point of going halfway, then coming back, then doing it all over again.

Nevertheless it caught on – albeit as an elitist pastime, practised exclusively by people with nasal voices and no chins. The splendidly egalitarian Swiss put a stop to that when Zurich engineer Erich Konstam arrived in Davos in 1934 and invented the cheap-to-install drag lift (see T-Bar) – the only form of uphill transportation designed with the explicit purpose of jettisoning its passenger without warning.

How Skiing Spread

It is generally accepted that mass labour migrations from Scandinavia during the 19th century account for the spread of skiing in America, Australia and New Zealand. This does not, however, account for how it spread to Morocco, India, Japan and Chile – but let's not be picky. A Norwegian introduced skiing to Australia for fun in 1861 and founded the Kiandra Club. But skiing had a more practical purpose in America. In California there was a skiing postman who delivered the mail over the Sierras in the 1850s. In Telluride, Colorado, on payday at the 'Tomboy' mine 3,000 feet above the town, the Finns and Swedes would strap on makeshift skis with grim determination and infuriate their co-workers by getting down to the 12 brothels before them.

SKI TERRAIN

Slopes and Grading

Slopes are called slopes or 'runs' or 'pistes' in Europe, 'trails' in America, and whatever anybody feels like calling them in Australia and New Zealand. People new to skiing will be relieved to discover that there are different gradients of slopes on a skiing mountain. They range from 'easy' to 'absurdly dangerous', and are graded by colour according to their degree of difficulty. Thus a 'green' slope is perceived to be easy, a 'blue' is less easy, a 'red' is less easy still, and a 'black' is no place for bluffers.

All runs have 'piste-markers' – appropriately coloured signs ingeniously placed to cause maximum obstruction. Black runs often have additional signs bearing the legend 'For experts only'. These signs generally prove irresistible to people who fondly imagine themselves to be experts but aren't. On no account fall victim to the same temptation. If the opportunity arises, there may be possibilities when nobody is looking to paint a blue sign black and transplant the 'experts only' sign to a blue run. Later, you can plunge past them shouting bravely "Geronimo!" to your startled friends.

In America they don't have red runs. It might have something to do with an unhappy association with the colour of blood. Their absence is compensated for by black runs which in Europe would be graded as red. To complete the American picture there are two types of black run – 'single' and 'double' diamonds. The double diamonds are the ones to avoid. But note that in some resorts they have two types of green and blue, also graded by diamonds. Only be seen on double diamonds of either.

All this subtle grading around the world is geared

towards the laudable objective of steering the right level of skier to the right part of the mountain. This in turn is meant to minimise the risk of injury and ensure that happy, carefree beginners and intermediates have a wonderful time without being flattened by 'experts' carving a swathe of human destruction down the mountainside.

This does not explain why most injuries and collisions occur on the easiest slopes. One possible explanation is that blues and greens are generally crowded with skiers concentrating so hard on staying upright they fail to notice where they are going. Another is that black and red runs generally intersect with blues and greens at the precise point guaranteed to cause maximum carnage.

Note for black-run skiers: it is generally fairly safe to flatten novices and children. It is never safe to flatten American lawyers or their families – not even when it's their fault.

Piste and Off-piste

The terms 'on piste' and 'off piste' have delighted headline writers for years. 'Piste-off' is a favourite for ski journalists trying to be witty about some calamity which has taken place on their 'familiarisation visits' (free ski trips). This usually has something to do with having to pay for their own drinks.

In fact, skiing 'on-piste' involves staying on marked runs which have been prepared ('groomed' in America) and made safe by 'piste-bashers' or 'sno-cats', machines which look like a cross between a tank and a combine-harvester, and which emit a bleeping noise to warn skiers of their presence: a noise invariably turned off when they approach blind bends.

Piste-bashers, and other assorted snow-grooming machinery, earned a certain notoriety in *On Her Majesty's Secret Service* when James Bond ski-jumped over one and the baddy following him didn't. There followed a great deal of grinding and squirting of blood and gristle which had cinema audiences around the world stamping their feet and applauding. Ever since this, drivers of these sinister machines behave as if they have a licence to mince.

After piste-bashers have done their worst, the surface is left like corrugated iron and is about as easy to ski on. That is why many people prefer to ski 'off-piste' ('off-limits' in America) – that part of the mountainside which is ungroomed, unmarked, largely unskied and frequently prone to avalanches, and if it's a glacier, crevasses. An increasing number of skiers would prefer to take their chances with these natural hazards rather than take on four tons of metal and a magi-mix.

Serious skiers never admit to skiing on piste, unless as a means of getting off-piste. If you happen to be on your way to ski off-piste, make great show of the fact to on-piste skiers by shouting to no-one in particular: "Franz. Have you got a spare pair of powder-straps?"

Moguls

Moguls are big bumps in the snow. In America they are called, with admirable inventiveness, bumps. They are caused by successive skiers turning in the same spot pushing the snow into hard, compact piles. If you hit one of these piles at speed, you will soar about 20 feet into the air before landing on your back with your ski in your ear. It is difficult to pretend that you did this on purpose.

There is a certain type of skier who claims to 'love' moguls. Nobody loves moguls, unless they are bluffing, in which case they must be accorded proper respect. This means that you must love them too. When you fall over, claim an old ligament rupture (see Injuries) prevented you from "achieving full absorption".

Paths

Paths are generally liberally strewn with rocks and black ice. On one side they have jagged cliff walls which invite your close attention; on the other side they have vertiginous drops through more rocks and splintered conifers. The splintering was caused by skiers.

Take careful note of where paths are and try to plan a route which avoids them. This is important, because everyone's natural inclination on a path is to adopt the snow-plough position, drag their poles between their legs, and whimper loudly. Bluffers cannot afford to be seen doing this.

Instructors will tell you that it's all about psychology and that the secret with paths is to pretend they're not there. Ignore them. They don't get caught in the conifers.

Piste Maps

Nobody has yet invented a piste map which returns to its original folds. In America they are called 'trail maps' and have up to 148 folds. These are the most advanced types of all and were allegedly invented by Rubik. Not even he can solve their limitless capacity to outwit.

Piste maps are supposed to show skiers where to go in clear, comprehensive, cartographical detail. Thus they bear little relation to the mountainside. In unfamiliar territory it is wise to allow someone else to take the initiative in guiding; then scoff mercilessly when all of you get lost.

Vertical Drops

An arresting feature of mountainous terrain, the term vertical drop actually describes two different things:

1. What will happen if you fail to stop at the edge of a sheer cliff face;

2. The distance in height between the top ski 'station' and the bottom (usually the resort).

For some reason the latter usage greatly exercises putative experts. Venture knowledgeably therefore that the biggest 'vertical' in the Alps is down the Vallée Blanche from L'Aiguille du Midi to Chamonix (approximately 2,750 metres or nearly two vertical miles); and in the Rockies, Blackcomb to Whistler (approximately 1,600 metres) known as The Vertical Mile.

Don't expect to survive a vertical drop of the first sort much over 10 metres.

CLOTHES AND EQUIPMENT

What you wear when you are skiing, or, more importantly, when you are not skiing but hanging around trying to look as if you are about to, is an intrinsic part of successful bluffing.

Zips, buckles, epaulettes, superfluous pockets, pockets on pockets, braid, fur and loud insignia combine to deliver a compelling and unmistakable message. They have the same effect as a neon sign flashing the words: 'This person cannot ski.'

The wise are not seduced by fashion mores and know the value of eschewing glitz and wearing old, suitably battered ski-clothes. Onlookers will immediately leap to the conclusion that you have been skiing for years. A useful role model for bluffers is the character played by Kirk Douglas in *The Heroes of Telemark* who sported a terrific blue anorak and a leather belt with grenades hanging off it. The grenades are not *de rigueur* unless you find yourself skiing in the Lebanon.

Those who are fortunate enough to have ancient skiing relatives could profit from investigating attics and old trunks. Nothing cuts a finer dash on the slopes than the original Golden Age of Skiing look, popular in the 1920s – best exemplified by Oliver Reed's character in the film *Women in Love*.

If all else fails, there is a ready-made and little known market for authentic-looking second-hand ski wear and – this is the clever part – you get to look like even more of an expert when you wear it. Many local instructors and guides are required to change their ski apparel every season, and therefore have trunkloads of the stuff lying around at home. Utterly baffled as to why anybody should be interested in their old ski clothes, they are easily persuaded to part with their soiled Gore-tex for bargain prices. Often they omit to take off their official badges, which means that you can masquerade as an expert as long as you don't go anywhere near their resort again. Or any slope anywhere.

A bewildering amount of nonsense is talked about skis, bindings and poles. This is therefore fertile territory for bluffers, but it is an area where a comprehensive knowledge of ski-talk is desirable.

Skis

Skis used to be made out of wood but are now made from an apparently infinite variety of materials with zappy names. All new skis boast the most remarkable technological advances ever achieved in the history of modern science. This must be true because upwards of 2,000 new models come on to the market every season and they all claim to render last year's skis obsolete – a sound enough argument for never buying new skis, and renting and ruining somebody else's.

Beware ski salespeople who know their stuff or sound as if they do. A typical conversation in a ski shop will go something like this:

Prospective purchaser (*modestly*): Can you recommend an 'all-round' ski for someone of average ability?

Salesperson: Lucky you came in today Sir/Madam. We've just laid our hands on the only pair of the Bionic-Zelcron Turbo Ex-plosion Ultima left in the world. It's unquestionably the best ski ever made.

Prospective purchaser (*interested*): I see. Why?

Salesperson (*taking a deep breath*): Unlike any other ski ever made, this latest Ultima has a Zelcron multi-layer vacuum sandwich construction ensuring maximum torsional rigidity yet balanced longitudinal flex, coupled with a Ketone-Kevlar microcell core, Z900 graphite base, V12 tapered torsion box, asymmetric gate deflector, trapezoid sidewalls, directional dampers, and an ultra-slim slalom sidecut which – all in all – will guarantee that Sir/Madam instantly becomes just about the best skier in the world. These babies will cut through concrete.

Prospective purchaser: Hmmm. Have you got them in pink?

Salesperson: Of course. Sir/Madam shows excellent taste. That will be £650 please.

Ski salespeople are fluent in 'ski-tech' in at least ten languages. Take careful note of what they say and repeat it *ad nauseam* when defending your particular choice. In fact, in most cases, the choice is determined by aesthetic considerations. Modern skis bear the most extraordinarily vulgar graphics. In a rare exception to the 'non-neon' rule, be as vulgar as you can afford to be in this department – as long as they don't have 'turbo' written on them anywhere.

There are only three things you really need to know about downhill skis:

1. That there should be two of them (unless you happen to be one-legged).

2. That they should match (not essential, but desirable).

3. That they should move forward when you stand on them pointing downhill.

But there are other important little titbits which can be dropped carefully into the conversation to show your mastery of the subject. Foremost amongst these is the uncontestable fact that skis are either 'hard' or 'soft' or somewhere in between. A hard ski is difficult to bend, a soft ski is not.

16

The enquiring skier will demand to know why there should be a difference. This has something to do with how a ski distributes its load along its 'camber' and how this affects its ability to turn. Simply remember that a hard ski distributes the weight of the skier evenly along its length, thus making it better for skiing hard snow on the piste.

In soft snow it is desirable for the tip to 'float', so a soft ski which concentrates the load in the ski's midsection is apparently better for turning. There is a useful mnemonic to aid memory here: 'Soft snow, soft ski. Hard snow, hard ski.' It is the basis of all ski technology.

There is a time-honoured way of testing ski-stiffness which may well impress bystanders. Hold the ski upright, put one foot against the bottom and, holding it by the middle with one hand, pull the top towards you with the other. This will show how flexible it is in the unlikely event that anybody is interested in knowing. If it snaps in half it clearly wasn't worth having.

'Edges' – the sharp metal bits on the side of the ski which grip the snow – are also something with which one should be familiar. If they are not sharp, they will not work. If they don't work, you will fall over. It is important that they be sharpened for effective 'edging' and so that you can 'carve' proper turns (see Technique) and stay upright as much as possible. A useful knack for gauging the right degree of sharpness is to run a fingernail across them. If a bit of nail is shaved off, things are fine. If not, you have a valid excuse for sliding uncontrollably about the mountainside. Claiming to have 'blunt edges' is a valid excuse for most forms of skiing ineptitude.

Another way to blame your skis for your semipermanent prostration is to claim that their 'soles' or 'bases' are gouged, or rough, or not properly waxed.

There may, surprisingly, be some element of justification in this claim. Worn running surfaces will adversely affect performance, so take no chances and get your skis fully 'tuned' as soon as you can – though never admit to having had a 'tuning', in case it makes absolutely no difference to your skiing. Having the base waxed tends to alarm many skiers who imagine that a more 'slippery' ski will be more difficult to control. In fact, the reverse is true – so you can wax away to your heart's content and convince yourself that your skiing is improving as a result.

The right length of ski is also a critical area. It is tempting to assume that length is somehow proportional to ability, and a common mistake is to buy or rent the longest ski in the shop. This is probably because the longer the ski is, the faster it goes. But however strong the temptation to demand a '210' (the longest non-competition size), resist it if you're planning to survive until après-ski.

Skis over 200cm should only be skied on by heavy experts, or by people who aren't planning to turn, or stop, at any stage of their descent. Those who have always instinctively felt that a shorter ski would be more suited to their level of incompetence can opt for 'carving' skis, also known as 'shaped', 'hourglass' or 'parabolics'. Carvers, which now account for nearly 100% of all new ski production, are wider at the tip and tail than conventional skis, up to 30cm shorter and thus a lot easier to manoeuvre. About time too. Designed to take the effort out of 'carving' a turn, they are a godsend to skiers who never quite come to terms with the concept of making any sort of turn in the first place.

Finally, the way skis are carried says much about their carrier. There is only one proper way to carry skis, and that is base to base, over one shoulder, with the tips pointing towards the ground. This looks better than any other way. There is no other reason for it.

Bindings

Bindings are the devices which hold the boots on to the ski. As long as they are in reasonable condition, there is very little to choose between them in terms of how they will affect performance. The most important function they have is to 'release' the ski when the skier is cartwheeling gracefully down the slope. If they do not release the ski, you will be unable to put any weight on your leg(s) for about three months.

In common with skis, bindings have developed their own arcane vernacular. Thus, if you are planning to buy some, you will hear a great deal about equalisers, inclined pivots, upper boot radius, lateral elasticity, power relays, anti-friction devices, and cam triggers.

Feel free to bandy these terms about; most skiers haven't an inkling what they mean either. The only bits of the binding you should be able to recognise are the 'toe units', 'heel units' and 'brakes'. The only term you actually need be familiar with is 'binding'.

The toe unit holds or releases the front of the boot, the heel unit does the same to the rear, and the brakes stop the ski skidding off down the mountain when it falls off. The brakes have absolutely nothing to do with slowing the rate of descent; that is only achieved by proper 'edging'. Or by colliding with a stationary object.

You are advised not to get too carried away with your expertise on bindings matters, and certainly not to the extent of tampering with the binding 'setting' yourself. This should be adjusted by someone who knows what he or she is doing. There is no need to admit to knowing nothing about how to adjust them yourself. Simply say, if asked, that you haven't got the right 'tool', and that for 'safety reasons' you prefer not to ski with bindings that haven't been tested on a 'torque' gauge – sinister-looking machines with clamps, mechanical twists and computer printouts.

Try to adopt one necessary habit before slotting into your bindings. Always tap the sole of the ski boot hard with your ski pole to dislodge compacted snow or mud. There is probably a safety reason for this but, more importantly, experts generally do it, so why shouldn't you?

Poles

Poles are what skiers call the long, spindly sticks which they carry with them on the slopes, and sometimes remember to 'plant' in the snow. Never call them sticks, nor leave them in the snow on the rare occasions you remember to plant them.

Like skis, poles are usually made of some fabulously advanced scientific material. They are made up of three component parts: the 'shaft', the 'grip' or handle, and the 'basket'. The basket is probably the most interesting part, because it not only has a useful function (to prevent the pole burying itself up to the hilt in the snow), but also because its name is frequently forgotten.

Handles come in a variety of 'sculpted', 'notched' or 'protective' shapes. The shape isn't remotely important. However, try to get hold of a pole with a 'shock absorber' between its handle and shaft, and insist they "really do make a difference on compression turns".

Shafts should be bent as soon as possible. This not only shows you have been 'planting' them often and hard, but that you have experienced a few spectacular crashes. Bending a pole can either be achieved by using your knee as a brace, by buying them ready-bent (called 'corrective angles'), or by falling on them.

Boots

Notwithstanding their unmanoeuvrability and the fact that they smell worse than an old mackerel after a day's skiing, ski boots are vital pieces of equipment. Unfortunately.

It has to be conceded, however, that they offer all the buckles, knobs, flashes, clips and levers the discerning foot-fetishist requires – none of which will single out the wearer as a person of questionable taste.

Ski boots fall into three categories: the alarming-sounding 'rear entry', the more innocuous sounding 'mid-entry' and the traditional 'front entry'. Rear-entries used to be fashionable but no longer are, mid-entries are for people who know no better, and front-entries are favoured by experts, professionals and racers. For this reason front-entries must also be favoured by you. The price you will have to pay is in loss of comfort, but as all boots have the comfort characteristics of a heavy duty industrial clamp, this is unlikely to be much of a sacrifice.

Front-entry skiers will need to point out the advantages of tightly fitting 'shells', increased control, and efficient energy transmission between shell and ski. Dismiss rear and mid-entries disparagingly as boots for "recreational skiers who prefer comfort to control". Front-entries have lots more clips and fiddly bits, essential, you will explain, for 'fine-tuning'.

It has been known for a certain type of hopelessly transparent ski bluffer to blame his or her boots for a chronically embarrassing inability to stay upright. Pointing accusingly at the offending items, they will say: "I just can't get enough flex." This sort of behaviour doesn't convince anyone. On the other hand, a boot of the wrong size can quickly render you unable even to think about blame.

Ski boot pain enters a different dimension of suffering. Chafed calves, bloodless toes, suppurating blisters, mind-numbing cramps, bruises on bruises, and toe-nails which curl up like poppadoms are something every skier will endure at some time – and those are some of the more bearable privations. If you invest in only one item of ski wear equipment make sure it's a ski boot which fits.

There is no such thing as a comfortable ski boot; just concentrate on finding one which doesn't make you pray for an early death. The admission of ski boot agony suggests the probability of inexperience. Experts never whinge about their boots.

Those just starting out should rent their boots to begin with and have no compunction about taking them back to the shop at the first sign of distress. Try out every pair in the resort, and if you find one that suits, sell everything you own to acquire it.

Bags

For those committed enough to skiing to buy their own boots and skis, there are certain guidelines to follow about the choice of luggage which contains them. If you are unable to find something pre-worn, send newly purchased bags to yourself via the Royal Mail – a parcel service which has perfected the means of achieving an instant 'distressed' look.

Original canvas and leather bags, proudly exhibited by descendants of Golden Age skiers, are at an absolute premium and cannot be purchased for realistic prices. If, by dint of extraordinary good fortune, you come across some which are unwanted – buy or purloin them immediately. They will ensure admiring glances for ever.

Once acquired, festoon your ski and boot bags with luggage labels suggesting that you have skied in fashionable or exotic places. If check-in staff have the bad manners to rip off superfluous labels, ensure that you have a back-up supply. This can easily be augmented by searching airport concourse floors.

Vital-to-be-avoided Impedimenta

There are certain basic rules for bluffers to observe. Never wear:

1. A bobble hat unless you are a complete novice, or a buffoon, or an instructor who wants to give the impression that he is above fashion considerations.

2. Racing pants if you have a large behind. Small children will point and snicker. So will most adults.

3. Salopettes (similar to dungarees) if you are afflicted with an excessive girth. They rarely have belts to restrain the stomach. Furthermore, they present special difficulties when visiting the lavatory. Horrifying stories abound of what ends up in the bib by mistake.

4. White pants (see slush), or all white (not easy to see on the slopes) unless you want to pass yourself off as a member of Der Alpen Korps. The advantages of professed membership of this august and glamorous body (which got soundly whacked by the Heroes of Telemark) are significantly outweighed by the tendency of every other skier on the mountain to ski into you at speed.

5. Chicken-lickin' type peaked balaclavas, baseball caps with gold-embossed laurel leaves on the peak or flying helmets.

6. Neon-coloured sun cream.

7. Backpacks which look like small furry animals.

8. Resort badges.

9. Headbands with christian names on the front (especially 'Adolf' or 'Trudl').

LIFTS AND QUEUES

There is a basic Newtonian logic to skiing: you have to go up before you can ski down. Going up involves a variety of forms. Take careful note of each because some knowledge of ski-lifts is essential for all-round dissembling.

Cable Cars

Called 'téléphérique', 'seilbahn' or 'funivia' in the Alps, and 'trams' in America, the cable car has queues at both ends and should be avoided by claustrophobics. They should also be avoided first thing in the morning by anyone with an aversion to body odour, boiled eggs, flatulence, acne, aftershave, and intimate physical contact with strangers.

They are at their most crowded first thing in the morning. Often they are also very busy last thing in the afternoon when there is either no other way to the bottom, no snow, or people can't be bothered to ski any more. On these occasions they are even more of an olfactory endurance test than in the morning.

Experienced skiers will demonstrate their superior knowledge of these things by always being first or last in and standing by the door (there are usually doors on both sides). That way they are supposed to have a 50 per cent chance of getting off first. Don't believe a word of it; only one door opens at a time – always the one furthest away from you.

Funiculars and Mountain Railways

Funiculars are dependent on cables to pull one up while another is coming down. They differ from cable cars in so far as they are either on the ground, or under the ground. This makes them popular with skiers who don't care to be dangled above the ground.

Traditionalists can say that nothing beats the old 'cog' and 'rack and pinion' mountain railways in Switzerland which go up impossible gradients painfully slowly. The steepest rack railway in the world is up Mount Pilatus near Lucerne, but you would be advised not to talk too authoritatively about the skiing at the top. There isn't any.

Gondolas

Gondolas are probably the most comfortable and convenient form of mountain transport. Like chairs, skiers are always guaranteed a seat – but unlike chairs skiers don't die of exposure on the way.

Gondolas have a man in a stripey T-shirt on board singing 'O sole mio', but that's only in Venice. On mountains they have up to six skiers staring silently out of the window and pretending the others aren't there – unless they're all friends with each other, or Americans. In America gondolas are called 'bubbles' because they're shaped like them. State confidently that gondolas are the best form of mountain lift. Only environmentalists will disagree.

Chairlifts

Chairs range from ancient one-seaters to 'high speed detachable quads'. Many skiers are understandably worried by the 'detachable' bit, but apparently it has something to do with a device for temporarily detaching them from the cable so skiers can get on and off easily. Gondolas have these as well. Despite this thoughtfulness all chairs are designed to smack into the back of your legs just above the ski boot and cause you to squawk involuntarily and fall backwards on to the seat.

You are required to keep your skis on for the duration of the journey. This small detail is largely academic because they always come off when you collide with your fellow passengers in the scramble to get off. Fight tooth and nail for the outside seat and ski off at an acute angle at the top to avoid trouble. Avoid getting on chairlifts with Americans (difficult in America) because they always tell you their life story. When the lift gets stuck, there's no escape.

T-Bars

T-Bars are, unquestionably, the most irksome form of transport ever devised. They first made their appearance simultaneously in Davos in Switzerland and Zurs in Austria. The Swiss and Austrians must never be forgiven for their folly. T-Bars are shaped like an upside down letter 'T'. They tow two skiers – each with one half of the cross bar wedged into some part of their lower anatomy. No two skiers are ever the same size which renders balance virtually impossible and ensures that all four skis will veer off in different directions.

There is one absolute certainty about T-Bars. When they finally eject you, they will do so in the most difficult terrain on the mountain. And that's no place to be with a stranger when it's your fault you both fell off.

Button Lifts

Button lifts are better than T-Bars because they take only one person at a time, and the soup-plate sized 'button' between the legs is easier to keep in place. Beginners will very quickly learn not to sit down on the soup-plates ('platters' in the US, 'pomas' in the Alps). They present different problems for men and women. Women should be wary of button lift attendants with a glint in the eye, which invariably means they will find a hand between the button and their buttocks.

Men should be wary for the same reason but should also be prepared for the pole to be yanked smartly upwards into their gonads. For some reason this provides lift attendants with considerable amusement. Males should grit their teeth and allow their eyes to water without saying a word.

Lift Passes/Attendants

Lift passes (tickets in the US) are the accepted way of paying for the lift. In most Alpine resorts the passes are computer coded, requiring them to be fed into a machine. These rarely work, necessitating a bad-tempered lift attendant to come out of his hut and shout at you. This usually has the effect of rousing the 200-strong queue behind to shout at you as well. Try to maintain a dignified silence in these circumstances.

Never wear your pass on elastic around your neck. One of the many ways lift attendants amuse themselves is by extending the elastic to its full length and catapulting the pass back into your eye.

It's as well to be aware of certain fundamental axioms about different country's 'lift systems' and their attendants:

Switzerland: Lift systems like their trains – fast, safe, efficient, often ingeniously tunnelled. Not always ingeniously linked. Attendants smart, brusque and stony-faced. They're wondering why if all Swiss are supposed to be rich, they aren't.

France: Lift system over-developed to the point of irresponsibility. De Gaulle's fault. Extraordinarily convenient, often leaving within inches of one's front door. Cleverly linked. Attendants have a serious attitude problem.

Austria: Lift systems usually involve long walks out of town. Keeps towns and villages nice and unspoilt, but tough on the feet. Methodical, worthy, reliable. Reputed to be bought second hand from the Swiss. Too many T-Bars. Attendants usually Australian.

Italy: Lift systems suspect. Mussolini's fault. Either extraordinarily ambitious and high-tech, and therefore unreliable; or primitive, and therefore unreliable. Much of lift superstructure reputed to be bought third hand from the Austrians. Attendants irrepressibly cheerful and utterly unreliable. Hands everywhere.

Eastern Europe: Lift systems antiquated, slow and dodgy. Lenin's fault. Reputed to be bought fourth hand from the Italians. Cable car in Poland needs to be booked a month in advance. Attendants charming, helpful. Keen to sell you caviar and currency.

America: Lift systems fast and comfortable, but too dependent on chairs. Not many chairs have safety bars.

Not always too cleverly linked. Attendants greet you like old friends. Always say 'How's it goin'?' followed by 'Have a good one'. It is sometimes temptin' to insert a ski-pole where the sun don't shine.

Queue Etiquette

The majority of continental Europeans act as if queues don't exist. This is an important point to note because the right response to queue-barging is not to foam conspicuously at the mouth, but to shake the head with an air of weary resignation. This proves to your companions that you have been in this situation many times before, and accept that confrontation is not the answer.

If you are feeling particularly bold, you can make great play of the queue-barger's churlishness by exclaiming in a loud voice: "Stand back. This person is in a hurry. Let him/her through because clearly he/she has something very important to do." It won't make any difference but you'll feel a lot better. Queue-bargers do not understand sarcasm, because they are not very intelligent. Generally they have very low foreheads and very long arms. They tend to be French, German, or possibly Swedish in which case they will almost certainly be drunk. Never American. In Europe, Americans will self-consciously stand aside for hours at a time, waiting for a lift attendant to tell them it's their turn.

If a queue-barger is behaving so badly that something simply has to be done, follow him or her very closely until you are both deep in the core of the heaving scrum. Position the point of your pole carefully over one of their binding releases and press downwards. If you have the opportunity, release both. The result, when they push forward towards the lift, is invariably satisfying. Even if they manage to get on the tow bar or chair, the ski will almost certainly fall off – and nobody looks too smart with one ski on.

If, in the scrum, the same should happen to you, there is regrettably very little you can do to keep your dignity intact. The only slim chance of coming through it with some credit is to pretend you did it on purpose, but this calls for bluffing skills of the highest magnitude and requires a prolonged amount of acrobatic clowning – a type of slapstick humour that continental Europeans are unaccountably partial to. If you can carry it off successfully, you may even be able to supplement your holiday budget by passing around your hat. Do not, however, expect too much from the Germans. Most of them will have taken advantage of the diversion to move a hundred yards ahead.

Skiing under Chairlifts

The best advice about skiing under chairlifts is: don't. Skiers on chairlifts take an unhealthy interest in skiers beneath them, and actually urge them to fall over. Often you will fall over because you will be aware that you're being closely watched and will therefore be keen to impress.

Never, ever try to impress people on a chairlift. Even if you succeed in skiing passably well, your efforts will be sneeringly dismissed as showing off. If you fall over, you will earn about as much sympathy as a fillet steak could reasonably expect from a rottweiler.

If you do find yourself skiing under a chairlift, wait until someone worse than you comes by. Ski as close to them as prudency allows and, if you think you can get away with it, pretend you are teaching them.

SURVIVING

Avalanches

The thing you really need to know about avalanches is that they aren't called the 'white death' for nothing. Having brought up the subject, sooner or later someone will ask you if you have been caught in one. If your audience is not co-operating, say something rhetorical like: "Believe me. An avalanche is no laughing matter. I... no, perhaps it's better left unsaid."

When pressed, pause, and gaze stoically into the distance. If you can manage it without dribbling, allow your bottom lip to quiver slightly. After a suitably pregnant silence, say softly, "It's not easy to talk about." This is true of course, because you know absolutely nothing about it. Follow this by saying enigmatically: "Did you know that an airborne powder snow avalanche can travel at speeds of up to 190 miles an hour? That's not too easy to keep ahead of – even for me."

If this doesn't have them marvelling continue with: "A block of wet snow three feet square weighs about three-quarters of a ton. Imagine the weight of something the size of a football pitch coming down the mountain after you." As you say this, rub your thighbone ruminatively and resolutely refuse to take the matter further. If you really want to push your luck say: "I was one of the lucky ones. But I can never ski the Widowmaker again."

There are two basic forms of avalanche which you might want to pretend to know about – 'loose snow' and 'slab' avalanches. Neither is much fun. If you hear an avalanche (interesting paralysing effect) you will usually be safe in saying "Sounds like a slab". If, on the other hand, there has recently been a fresh 'dump' of snow and you're not sure what sort it is, try:

31

"Sounds like an avalanche" and get down the mountain as quickly as possible.

A **loose snow** avalanche can be caused by the weight of a heavy fall of new 'powder' snow on a very steep slope, or by 'wet' snow which has thawed and not 'bonded' properly with a fresh fall. A **slab** avalanche (the most common) happens when a fracture line breaks and releases a huge amount of snow in blocks in a sort of domino effect. It is usually caused by wind, and not the sort you will be short of if it hits you.

Glaciers

At some stage you will need to pretend you know something about glaciers. Glaciers are moving rivers of ice which pulverise everything in their path. Fortunately their progress is generally slow – no more than an inch or two a day so that even the British Olympic team can keep ahead of them, but in Alaska and Iceland they can steam along at up to 15 feet an hour.

They start very high up the mountain above the permanent snow-line and are 'fed' by the permanent 'snow-fields'. They can be skied on with minimal risk if your guide (essential precaution) knows where the crevasses are. This is all you really need to know about glaciers apart from certain key words like 'seracs' (pinnacles of ice which form eye-catching sculptures), 'moraines' (the debris of crushed stone at the glacier's sides and end) and 'snout' (the front end). Familiarity with these terms will ensure instant respect from all who have the pleasure of listening to you.

For the more ghoulish, there are various stories about perfectly preserved mountaineers and skiers being disgorged by glaciers many years after their deaths. How this is supposed to happen if glaciers can reduce boulders to dust, nobody has satisfactorily explained. But it makes a good story.

Crevasses

Never claim to have fallen into a crevasse, not only because the chances of getting out alive are slim, and therefore people will be disinclined to believe you, but also because the reasons for falling in in the first place have more to do with negligence than fortitude. The best approach is to pretend that you risked your life rescuing some other poor fool who skied too close to one. So you will need to know what a crevasse is. This is the simple part.

Crevasses are big holes in a glacier caused by glacial movement and subsequent fractures in the ice. They are generally very deep (up to 200 feet) and always dangerous. They are also sometimes difficult to spot because their 'lips' are often concealed by snow. This means that, when the snow collapses beneath a skier's weight, the crevasse has a disturbing tendency to show its true contours rather suddenly – sucking anybody standing on top into its frozen depths. Hope of rescue is often futile because if the fall doesn't kill you, the intense cold probably will. Furthermore, most professional rescuers have a healthy respect for crevasses and prefer to stay a safe distance away.

If, however, you are determined to push your deceptive powers to the limit, explain that the victim was fortunate enough to land on a 'snow bridge' – a build-up of hard snow, spanning the crevasse. It is usually flimsy and therefore not to be relied on, so don't claim to have dropped fearlessly on to it, skis clamped firmly between your teeth. Waffle instead about ropes and crampons and painstaking precautions and first aid. With any luck your audience will fall asleep before they see through you.

Snow Storms

Also known as 'white-outs'. Cold, merciless, and unpredictable, they can reduce visibility to the end of your nose. When they occur, the best course is to follow your nose to the nearest mountain restaurant and wait until it blows over. With luck it won't and you can stay in the restaurant all night, later telling your friends that you had to dig a snowhole and survive for ten hours in freezing temperatures.

White-outs usually occur when you are stuck on a chairlift.

Being Stuck on a Chairlift

This is one of the coldest and most trying events you can experience. It is made marginally worse by being on the windward side or next to a garrulous American. Ways of passing the time include snapping off your frozen fingers and throwing them at lift attendants dithering about beneath.

Frozen Fingers

The time-honoured way of dealing with frozen fingers is to point them downwards and tap them against something to keep the blood flowing. Amazingly, it works.

Snow Cannons

These are artificial snow-making machines used by resorts with a dodgy snow record to cover a couple of square yards of barren, rocky piste.

How the snow is actually 'made' is anybody's guess, but it's supposed to have something to do with temperature and water pressure and underground reservoirs and so on.

What is important is knowing where they are likely to be sited. Rather like piste-bashers, snow cannons lurk round corners waiting for unsuspecting skiers to arrive before starting up. There is no recommended course to adopt when finding yourself skiing into a dense cloud of artificial snow. We suggest you close your eyes and pray.

Après-ski

Surviving après-ski is one of the most important parts of the skier's Survival Code. The term was invented by the French to describe that convivial part at the end of the day when skiers get together, have a few drinks, and then lie disgracefully about their skiing exploits. Unaccountably, the French then effectively abolished après-ski by building hideous Stalinist prison camps all over the French Alps making it impossible for anyone to enjoy anything. There are a few bars left in some of the concrete blocks, but the staff have been so brutalised by their environment that they can rarely do more than snarl.

Where après-ski still thrives (notably Austria and Italy) there are certain basic rules to observe:

1. Always ensure that one of your party remains sober enough to show the rest of you the way home.

2. Never urinate against a lamppost in freezing conditions (unless someone is prepared to detach you).

3. Avoid excessive intake of 'gluhwein' (a curious alcoholic cough mixture once described by a ski writer as 'a useful adhesive for securing a hairpiece').

Mountain Restaurants

Here everything costs up to three times as much as in the resort. A useful formula for calculating the percentage increase is: 50% for every 1,000 feet in altitude.

The best mountain restaurants are easily identified by the British, French, German and Italians engaged in pitched battles for tables and chairs on the sun terraces. Alliances are not always split on wartime lines, but expect the Germans to win (having previously bribed the restaurant staff to intervene on their behalf).

Mountain restaurants are also identifiable by large signs which read 'NO DRINK – NO WC'. Because there is never anywhere else to relieve yourself on the mountain, the cost of queuing to use the restaurant's only lavatory (in France, a hole in the floor) can be as much as the price of a Pschitt (see Glossary).

Altitude

Surviving the effects of increased altitude is relatively straightforward if you don't exert yourself. But since a skiing holiday is likely to be the only time of the year that you actually do exert yourself, the effects of altitude can be somewhat alarming. If you have ever witnessed a grounded fish gasping on a river bank, you will have some idea of what to expect at the end of your first mogul field. Sometimes it can be as bad as that just getting out of bed. This is especially true of America, where many of the Colorado resorts are located at about 9,000 feet.

Altitude 'sickness' is a common complaint amongst those who don't want to admit they are chronically unfit. But there are some advantages. For example, it doesn't require much alcohol to become completely incapacitated. This can result in significant savings.

Furthermore (and more importantly) the after effects are for some reason much more bearable.

There are two useful facts to have in store for altitude conversations:

1. Above 1,500 metres (4,500 feet), it takes twice as long to boil an egg.

2. Ultra violet intensity increases by 20% for every 1,500 metres of altitude, and snow reflects up to 85% UV radiation (a very good reason for religiously reapplying your total sunblock).

Blood Wagons

This is the cheerful name given to canvas hammocks slung between two wild-eyed stretcher bearers on skis. Those who have opted to take this alternative means of downhill transportation (often necessitated by injury) report that nine times out of ten they would prefer to suffer the injury again.

Blood wagon skiers (one at the front, one at the back, sometimes side by side if the one at the back is faster) are usually frustrated Olympic speed skiers. Like their heroes – they aim, point, gather speed, and refuse to turn (not even for rocks). Their sole objective is to cause maximum discomfort to the crippled passenger. They are remarkably proficient at their job.

Injuries

The most important thing to remember about ski-orientated injuries is that they should be described with lurid dispassion. An entirely imaginary shard of bone which once pierced your salopettes can be described in the most gory detail and at length – as long as the description is casually qualified by: "I'd just bought the bloody things as well."

There are certain basic injuries which every skier should claim to have suffered. The 'twisted knee' is perhaps the most common. Fifty per cent of snow skiing injuries involve the leg, and half of these involve the knee. To describe your real or imagined injury as a mere 'twist' is to waste a glorious opportunity for some shameless bluffing. A "partial rupture of the anterior cruciate ligament" is what should be said instead. Only orthopaedic surgeons know what this means if anything so, unless your audience is comprised of genuine bone boffins, you should be on safe ground.

If pressed for further details gabble about white fibrous tissues, inflammation, femurs, tibias and how you suffered it by landing heavily on a rock to avoid a small child. "Sudden deceleration," you will say sadly. "It always gets the old cruciate."

If your injury is minor, resist the temptation to play it up too much because this will not only tempt fate but you are bound to forget to limp at a crucial moment. The best course is to say: "I think I got away with it – this time." If, on the other hand (and heaven forbid), it is major, play it up with the crashing accompaniment of a full symphony orchestra. The right approach is to say "It'll hurt like hell, but I'm not going to let that mountain defeat me." Tears will spring to your audience's eyes, and with luck yours as well, followed by widespread admiration for being such a stalwart.

Other popular injuries are in the shoulder region. If you happen to land on the point of your shoulder, you will not need to bluff: the pain – or the memory of it – will be plain for all to see. But if you insist on pressing your luck, choose to have dislocated it in a spectacular crash, occasioned by consideration for the inexperienced. There is a very useful word to remember in this context, viz: "Damned thing 'popped' out. I was dragging my knuckles around the mountain like an orang-utan until a passing pisteur 'popped' it back in." 'Popping', therefore, is a vital part of any injured skier's vocabulary. It has the distinct advantage of suggesting pluck and fortitude in the face of adversity, and is guaranteed to turn any listener faint.

There is a useful piece of injury-suggestive equipment which you might consider acquiring – especially when you know that your lack of skiing ability is about to be exposed. The best ruse for continuing the bluff when all else fails is to invest in a high-tech surgical knee-brace. These make it impossible to ski with any degree of style, and also say a great deal about your extraordinary courage for skiing at all. If you want to look particularly stoical, invest in two – even if this does have the effect of making you walk like John Wayne.

What Injuries Not to Have

A bruised bottom – no matter how severe, is always a cause for mirth. Worse still, it suggests that you can't ski properly. A sprained thumb is also to be avoided. It hurts like blazes, renders your pole-planting all but impossible, keeps you awake at night, makes you very bad-tempered, and earns you no sympathy whatsoever.

TECHNIQUE

The first thing you need to appreciate about how to do it is that you are unlikely to learn anything from a book about how to pretend to be able to do it when you can't. One solution to the problem is to steer well clear of any situation where you might have to prove how advanced your 'technique' is to the people you have been bluffing.

This will be difficult at the best of times, not least because it means you won't be able to ski with your friends (the most likely victims of your delusions). A more expedient solution is to know something about the theory even if you haven't got a clue how to put it into practice. This will ensure that you can 'talk' a good bit about skiing – despite the fact that you spend conspicuously more time on your back than on your skis. You can always resort to our suggested catalogue of excuses (see injury, equipment, conditions, etc.) to explain why this is so.

The Theory

The basic theory of skiing technique is that once you have conquered your fear of the 'fall-line' you have essentially cracked the secret of how to ski. After that it is just a matter of refining your technique (i.e. 'looking good'). **Looking good** is the whole point of technique, although purists will tell you that 'control' is what it's all about.

Control is something that will be alien to most ski bluffers. Nonetheless, you must make stern and responsible noises about how vital it is for safe and effective skiing, and secretly strive to attain it. Exactly why it's so vital will become clear when you need to stop, or take evasive action – suddenly. This happens quite a lot.

The **fall-line** is the steepest, and thus the quickest, way down a slope. In other words, if you weren't planning on turning at any stage, this would be the route your skis would take you (assuming that you were still attached to them). Instructors and instruction books will tell you that fall-lines have nothing to do with falling over. If this is the case, you might legitimately ask "Why are they called fall-lines?"

Being told not to be frightened of the fall-line is akin to being told not to worry when you fall out of a light aircraft some distance above the ground. The shortest distance between the aircraft door and the ground is also called a fall-line, because that is the way you will fall. Your instinctive reaction when first looking down a fall-line on a mountain will be to imagine the 'no-parachute' scenario – and, therefore, to wish to give vent to your fear. Resist this impulse at all costs, especially if you have an audience. There are ways of coping with the fall-line:

The Snow-plough

This is not a heavy-duty farm implement but the method of controlling your rate of descent by forming your skis into a V-shaped wedge, with the tips forming a narrow head and the tails as wide apart as you can get them. The wider apart your tails, the slower you go – in theory.

Unfortunately, snow-ploughs are not very effective on steep fall-lines. They also have the singular disadvantage, from a skier's point of view, of suggesting to the world that you can't ski. It will be necessary, therefore, to adopt another technique for coping, for example:

Schussing

A 'schuss' is popular with those skiers with a 'let's melt mountain' mentality. It involves keeping the skis together, aiming the tips down the fall-line, and hoping for the best. If it is a particularly steep fall-line, you might yell with false bravado, "See you in hell", before setting off. Sometimes (most of the time) it is difficult to stop on a schuss. It is therefore important to determine whether or not there is a reasonably flattish bit at the bottom. If there isn't, think twice before going.

There is a special position to adopt in the schuss. It's a sort of crouch called a 'tuck' or an 'egg', where you bend down over the skis with your bottom in the air, your poles tucked into your armpits. It looks absurd, and it causes a peculiarly painful sensation in the thigh muscles. There must be good reason for doing it, like minimal wind-resistance, but the real reason probably has more to do with the fact that you will be that much closer to the ground when you fall over.

Edging

'Edging' is the term given to the practice of pressing the metal edges of your skis into the snow. If you don't want to go straight down the fall-line, you can stand at right angles to it with both your skis across the slope and their 'uphill' edges 'biting' into it. If they don't bite properly you will find yourself embarked on another method called 'side-slipping' (see below).

If they do bite properly, you will remain stationary – even (one is assured) on near-vertical slopes. Edging is therefore a useful technique to acquire, and to be familiar with as in: "Good to see your edging's coming along" or "Experts always ski on their edges" (except, of course, when they're schussing).

Having established the point of edges, the next stage is to see what happens when you change your right-angle position by a couple of degrees. If you point the tips of the properly edged skis uphill you will slide backwards, if you point them downhill you will slide forwards. The general idea, if you want to move, is to point them downhill. As yet there is no variant of the sport called 'skiing backwards' – unless you count freestyle.

Traversing

The actual movement of crossing a slope like this is called a 'traverse'. In theory it describes any manoeuvre where your skis follow any straight line other than the fall-line. Like edging, it is a useful technique to acquire. Ideally, you should be edging all the time you are traversing. It is the next quickest way to get down the mountain (apart from rolling).

At some stage your traverse will have to come to an end; otherwise you will traverse straight over a cliff or into a tree. The means of doing so is called:

Turning

Turning is fundamental to skiing – although many skiers (notably blood-wagon bearers, pigs-on-planks, and novices) disagree. A normal descent, unless it is a schuss, is a series of 'linked' turns. Or should be. Note that you never simply turn; you always 'carve' a turn.

Carving a turn takes many different forms:

The Snow-plough turn. On reflection snow-plough turns are rarely 'carved'; they are ploughed. The idea is that you put more weight on one ski than the other in the snow-plough position and, miracu-

43

lously, you turn in the opposite direction to the weighted ski. Exactly why this happens need not concern you. Just declare 'weighting' to be the basis of all turning technique.

The Stem turn. This is a snow-plough turn which starts and finishes with the skis together in a normal traverse position. You just have to remember to open or 'stem' them at the right moment, otherwise you might skip a lesson or two and do a 'parallel' turn by mistake. If you do manage a parallel turn by mistake, try to remember how you did it.

The Stem Christie. This takes its name from 'Christiania' which is what Oslo used to be called, and where the turn was invented. Essentially, it is a speeded-up stem turn with – and this is the tricky bit – the skis together when you reach the fall-line. This involves split-second weight transference, and a lot of 'sinking down', 'springing up' and 'angulation' to come out of the fall-line. If you haven't quite mastered it you 'hit' the fall-line and don't come out of it. Then you find yourself yelping and doing an involuntary schuss.

The Parallel turn. 'Skiing parallel' used to describe the practice of keeping your skis glued together throughout the entire turn. The few who managed to achieve this unlikely feat after years of determined endeavour are now told that the skis should be a hips-width apart instead of stuck together. This is conclusive proof of a worldwide conspiracy amongst ski instructors to redefine technique whenever they feel like it, thus ensuring a constant supply of work.

The Jet turn. The 'jet' turn sounds terrific and looks terrific. In essence it's a parallel turn with the skier sitting back – which is exactly what you are not supposed to do. It involves 'checking', 'anticipating', 'sinking', 'unweighting', 'braking' and 'carving'. All you have to remember is to do all these things in the space of about one-hundredth of a second. Simple really.

The Compression turn. Another name for colliding with a mogul, and discovering that your knees have been relocated two feet above your head. The technique employed necessitates appropriate 'absorption' of the bump. It was invented by the French, who insist on calling it an 'avalement' turn. Avalement means 'swallow' which is what you may do with your knees while attempting to execute this manoeuvre.

The Wedel turn. The art of linking very short parallel turns in a rhythmic up-down bouncing motion. The concept is that one turn flows directly into another in a rapid 'wagging' motion, with the upper body facing downhill all the time. 'Wedeling' comes from the German word 'wedeln' (to wag) and has nothing to do with how ski journalists cajole free meals.

The Jump turn. One which comes in handy on very steep slopes and in deep, heavy snow. It is often initiated from a stationary position, and requires both skis to turn in mid-air and face in the opposite direction. If the tips happen to cross in mid-execution, you may well engage in interesting acrobatics for the remainder of your descent.

The Carving turn. Turns on carving skis require a slightly difference technique. Unfortunately no-one (least of all instructors) can agree what it is. Thus you will hear lots of conflicting advice about 'rolling your ankles', 'even-weighting', and 'following your shoulders'. Ignore it all. Carving skis make whatever turn they feel like.

Side-slipping

Perhaps the most effective technique of all for dealing with the fall-line, especially for those who prefer not to schuss or turn. It involves a mixture of edging and 'flattening' the skis. When both skis are flattened together, they will slide sideways down the slope until the edges are 're-set'. For some unaccountable reason, when you reach the bottom in safety, friends gather around and chant 'chicken'. This is most unfair and confers a completely undeserved stigma on a perfectly valid means of descent.

Stopping

An oft-neglected technique which can involve a great deal of buttock-contact with the mountainside. There are other ways of executing a stop manoeuvre, like braking with your edges and pointing your ski-tips uphill, but nothing really beats the buttock routine for all-round style and effectiveness.

Preparation

This is something that skiers are supposed to do assiduously for three or more months before their holiday. It is also called 'exercise' or 'getting fit'. In reality, most skiers talk about it a lot but avoid doing anything about it with a determination which is quite uncharacteristic. A standard excuse is that you don't want to aggravate "your old ligament injury".

It will be tempting to maintain that you have never needed a lesson in your life. This is ill-advised, not least because it will lay you open to the entirely legitimate retort: 'Yes, it shows.' Instead, candidly admit that you had a lesson in the early days – just, of course, to learn the basics. Nobody need ever know that learning the basics took you up to ten weeks.

At ski school you will learn how to join up to 30 other people in following an instructor down a slope. The fact that 29 of them can't see what the instructor is doing is irrelevant.

Ski school is a useful way of meeting people, discovering (hopefully) that there are people worse than you, and confirming that few instructors speak intelligible English. Don't be surprised at 'imbecile' or 'idiot' when you admit to some confusion about what you are supposed to do. These are terms of affection in French, Scottish, German and Italian. Speed of comprehension depends upon whether you have private or group lessons. Reckon on one private lesson being worth about five group lessons. Take full advantage of this opportunity to learn the following basics: how to **stand**, how to **get up**, how to **turn** and how to **stop**.

This is all you really need to know apart from tips to cope with the following conditions:

Ice

There is no known technique for handling ice on the piste, and normal skiing procedures like edging have little effect. What happens when most skiers encounter it is that they have a panic attack, try to turn, and then perform a 'splits' routine. You will, of course, know better than to turn. You won't be on the slope in the first place.

Powder

This is the stuff you find off-piste – a place which bluffers talk about incessantly but where they rarely venture. All enthusiasts need to know that 'powder-skiing' is the next best thing to sex. Key words include 'exhilarating', 'floating', 'deep', 'virgin' and 'serpent trails'. The latter are what you will claim to have left behind you in 'virgin powder'. (The fact that your trail will look more like you've been dragging a fir tree should never be mentioned.)

When the question of how to do it comes up, you will need to know that a different technique is required. All you need to say is "It's all in the weighting", and promptly change the subject. Never admit to skiing on 'fat boys' – extra wide skis which bounce along on the surface of the snow and make it possible even for the perpendicularly challenged to powder-ski. Insist that 'fat-skiing' is cheating and potentially calamitous for purists, then hire a pair as soon as you can.

If you are imprudent enough to attempt powder-skiing on conventional equipment, remember one vital piece of advice. To save time looking for your skis in three feet of snow it's a good idea to carry a pair of 'powder straps' – lengths of elastic which attach skis to boots and strangle you in the avalanche you have just triggered. Even if you never have cause to use them, you can throw them casually on to the table in mountain restaurants and bars when you're sure someone is looking.

COMPETITIVE SKIING

All skiers are competitive, but some are more competitive than others. It's a good idea to know something about competition skiing, particularly ski racing, so that you can drop a few names and venture the odd informed opinion about the classic races.

Only three disciplines really count: downhill, slalom, and giant slalom.

Downhill

This is the most fun to watch, especially if you're one of those who slows down to get a closer view of a car crash. The courses are between two and three miles long for men, about two miles for women. Both will expect to finish in under two minutes at average speeds of 70mph for men and 60mph for women. Vertical drops range from 500 to 1,000 metres.

When contestants fly past (sometimes airborne for more than 50 yards at speeds of over 90 mph), no-one can hear them scream because spectators are required to shout "Hup! Hup! Hup!" (a curious exhortation considering that they are trying to come down).

Downhill racing is the most suicidal of the disciplines but success confers undreamt-of prestige for the winning survivor. Whole nations weep with pride, and clasp downhill champions to their bosoms (figuratively speaking) and think of them as favoured sons or daughters.

The British don't do this of course, because it is not in the national character. The fact that the British have never had a downhill champion has absolutely nothing to do with it.

Slalom

This is a race on a very steep, short, icy section of piste which requires men to pass between 55 to 65 gates, and women between 45 and 60. The idea is to see how many red and blue poles they can uproot, and who can do it the quickest. The race is run over two legs.

Giant Slalom

Similar to slalom, but run over a longer course at higher speeds. Two legs of about 90 seconds each. Even more contestants impale themselves than before.

Only three skiing competitions really count: the **Winter Olympics** (held every four years), the **World Championships** (held every two years), and the **World Cup** (every year) – the Grand Prix of ski racing.

The Olympic downhill is the big one, where one hundredth of a second can mean the difference between immortality and relative obscurity.

There are two great World Cup classics:

1. **The Hahnenkamm**. This is held in Kitzbuhel, Austria. It is so frightening that hardened racers have to be dragged kicking and screaming to the starting line. There they're pushed over a vertical drop, free fall for about ten seconds, and spend the rest of the course fighting to regain control of their skis (and their bowels).

2. **The Lauberhorn**. By comparison the Lauberhorn, held in Wengen (Switzerland), is a pleasant Sunday afternoon stroll – at 80 mph. The oldest of the courses, it has some infamous sections, amusingly named after scenes of great national disasters. (Never joke about Canadian Corner or Austrian Hole to ski racers from either country.) The celebrated Swiss skier Peter Mueller had a spectacular crash on the jump into the finish. He survived, but about ten hay bales were vaporised.

The other major World Cup races are held in Val d'Isère (France), Garmisch (Germany), Val Gardena (Italy) and Aspen (USA). They can be safely called "tough, but not too tough".

VARIANTS

Cross-country

The oldest form of skiing, this is variously known as 'Nordic' because the Nords invented it, 'langlauf' in German, 'ski de fond' in French, and 'sci di fondo' in Italian. Involving the use of a long, thin, curly ski, it feels similar to a fast walk with strips of fettucine attached to your feet. The movement has little in common with the technique for downhill skiing – excessive expertise in which is likely to prove to be a disadvantage. Bluffers will therefore enjoy a distinct advantage in mastering cross-country skiing.

Other points to note include the fact that you must wear a skin-tight, very shiny body-stocking to look the part, and best of all – if you should happen to take part in an event – you are actually expected to fall over at the finishing line in a state of total exhaustion.

Uphill

Otherwise known as ski-touring or ski-mountaineering this has been specifically designed for masochists, members of the SAS (same thing), and French Army conscripts (poor sods). It requires a level of physical fitness close to that expected of a double-marathon runner. It involves climbing up mountains with your skis on for hours on end – a feat only made possible by special bindings which allow the heel to lift out of the heel-unit, and 'skins' which are attached to the soles of the skis to prevent them sliding backwards. Skins used to be made out of seal hides, but are now made from something synthetic and prickly.

Ski-tourers like staying in remote mountain refuges and bluffing to each other that they're not close to death from excessive physical exertion.

Mono-skiing

This is neither skiing on your own because you can't allow your friends to see how inept you are, nor skiing on one ski because the other has fallen off. The term is used to cover the practice of skiing on a single broad ski with a dual binding which accommodates both feet side-by-side. Mono-skiers tend to plant their poles more viciously than duo-skiers; it's the only way they can keep their balance.

Snowboarding

Also known as 'surfing' or 'shredding', snowboarding is a cross between wave-surfing and mono-skiing – but without poles or sharks.

Snowboards always have 'turbo' written on them somewhere, and travel at speeds upwards of Mach 2. Snowboarders, or 'riders' (affectionately known by some skiiers as 'gays-on-trays') usually have long hair, sometimes fetchingly pony-tailed, and shout things like 'Awesome, Dude!' when they crash into you. This is just one example of a completely impenetrable language which all skiers will be required to learn fairly quickly. Within the next decade it is estimated that snowboarders will comfortably outnumber skiers.

Ski-birding

Ski-birders have wing flaps on their arms. Sometimes they have poles as well. They will flap their wings, doing a passable impression of those early aviators intent on proving that human flight didn't require an internal combustion engine. Sometimes they catch a thermal, and achieve an unexpected amount of uplift. Then they squawk just like birds, before plummeting impressively to the ground. Ski-birding is a hugely entertaining spectacle, and ski-birders everywhere are to be applauded for providing so much fun.

Short Ski/Bigfoot

These involve the use of truncated skis and, in the case of Bigfoot, wide tips with toes amusingly painted or sculpted onto them. The idea is that short skis are easier to control, and this is generally true except in a schuss when they slide around all over the place.

Short skis are still popular as a method of learning. The French have developed a teaching technique called Ski Evolutif which starts beginners on short skis, and gradually allows them to progress to mid-length skis. The Americans have a similar system ponderously called Graduated Length Method. Both insist they were first.

Telemarking

A cross between cross-country and downhill skiing, telemarkers ski downhill on cross-country skis. This requires a completely different turning technique which involves going down on one knee like Sir Lancelot. It takes its name from the Norwegian province of Telemark where it was invented. Colorado exponents of the art are called 'raisin-pickers'.

Freestyle Skiing

Freestyle is something few skiers do on purpose. It involves performing somersaults, aerobatics, ballet, spins, the splits, landing on your head – in fact all those manoeuvres which the average bluffer can expect to perform in a typical day on the piste.

SNOWCRAFT

Easy familiarity with different forms of snow is a useful bluffing device. Indeed, most skiers will be surprised to know that there is more than one type.

What 'sort' of snow it may be is determined by a number of factors including the temperature, the amount of water in the atmosphere, the wind speed at the time of the snowfall, and the changes it undergoes once it has landed. You can impress people hugely by 'examining' it, and pronouncing upon your findings.

The 'snowball' test is crucial here. You don't have to know what it is supposed to prove, but it has something to do with 'fusion'. If you can make a nice compact snowball, the snow is likely to be old; if it won't fuse at all, it's likely to be new. Of course, you could probably tell whether it's old or new by looking out of the window to see if it is snowing or not. But that's not the point. The point is that its 'age' says a lot about how it will ski and whether it is likely to avalanche. All snow can avalanche.

A big fall of new snow is called a 'dump'. If you call it anything else you reveal gross inexperience. If that should happen, you will need to gabble about:

Powder Snow – Fresh snow which hasn't begun to melt. It is dry, loose, and impossible to make into snowballs. It squeaks when you walk on it, and three or four inches of it on a 'firm base' is every skier's dream.

Hard-pack – Oldish powder snow which has been compressed into a hard, well-beaten surface by a piste-basher.

Spring Snow – Powder which has begun to thaw but is refrozen overnight into hard, granular particles.

Usually only found early in the morning towards the end of the season. Also known as 'corn' snow. Pretend to have risen at dawn "to look for it" (but remember only to search on south-facing slopes). The holy grail of snow until it warms up and turns into 'slush'.

Crust – An icy layer on top of powder, found off-piste. If thin and easily broken, it is said to be not too difficult. If it's thick and only breaks on turns, it is called 'breakable crust' which is one of the least attractive surfaces to ski on. Your ski will happily surge on ahead in the soft snow beneath it, but your boot will be required to act like a polar ice-breaker. For instant credibility claim that it causes you no real problems.

Porridge/mashed potato/Sierra cement – Thick, sticky, old snow in advanced state of decay. Difficult to turn on. Has a tendency to gather at the bottom of runs, or any other place where large numbers of people congregate to watch the carnage.

Yellow snow – Curious meteorological phenomenon found near lift attendants' huts, or mountain restaurants which restrict the use of toilets to customers only. Not to be investigated too closely.

CHOOSING A RESORT

Claim to be guided by three considerations:

1. **Altitude**

The higher the better. There is more snow at altitude.
You will know that the resort height is not as crucial as
the height of the 'top station', which should be well
above the tree-line. This needn't be the case in America
where the tree-line is twice as high as in the Alps.

If you want to be disparaging about somebody's
choice of resort it is usually safe to say: "Too low"
except in Colorado, parts of the Tarentaise, much of
Switzerland and around Mont Blanc.

2. **Tough skiing terrain**

Vital for bluffers – even if they have no intention of
going anywhere near it.

3. **Snow record and conditions**

You will be expected to know all about this. Current
conditions can be found in some newspapers throughout the season, or by spending a fortune ringing a
Snow-line. Historic conditions need only be alluded
to, but it is useful to be able to say "such-and-such
had 40 feet of snow last season".

Depth of snow is all-important. You must know that
12cm (5 inches) is the absolute minimum to ski on, but
considerably more than that is preferable as an ideal
'base'. Finally, 'direction of slopes' is a vital constituent.
Snow 'holds up' better on north-facing slopes than
south-facing ones (because they spend less time in the
sun). A surfeit of north-facing slopes in a resort is
therefore a good thing. But not if you want a suntan.

SKI TYPES

Bluffers must be able to recognise certain categories of other skier if only to confirm which are fellow bluffers and which are not.

The Mountain Legend

There is no terrain he hasn't skied, no skiing challenge he hasn't conquered, no crevasse he hasn't been in, no avalanche he hasn't 'raced', and no cliff he hasn't jumped. He skis in powder so deep he needs a periscope to see where he's going. He makes these outrageous claims in the absolute knowledge that no-one can refute them, because no-one has ever seen him ski. This is because he 'must ski alone': the danger gives him an adrenaline 'buzz'. He wears an avalanche transceiver on the outside of his suit – £700's worth of zips and buckles, guaranteed pristine at all times.

The Hot-Rod

He rarely skis because he can't afford to spend that long away from a mirror. He notches up female victims on his skis like a fighter pilot on his fuselage. If asked why he doesn't ski he will say that he's got 'bored' with it. In fact he could never get the hang of it. If a flea dived into his pool of skiing knowledge, it would break its neck.

The Snow-Kitten

Kittens hang around hot-rods looking thin and pained. This is because hot-rods don't pay them any attention and kittens don't know what else to do. Like hot-rods, they are keen on suntans and video bars and not too keen on snow. They are also keen on fur, Ferraris, fat wallets and people called Fabio. They aren't too clever though: they usually fail to notice that Fabio hasn't got any money.

Kittens could probably ski quite well if they could direct their formidable single-mindedness to learning. But they can't see the point. Their skills extend only as far as their appearance. This is invariably chic, expensive, and utterly useless as a means of weather protection.

The Pig-on-Planks

PoPs are notoriously violent: with little provocation they would stick a ski in your mouth – sideways. They tend to have thick necks and no brains: they can often be seen trying to figure out how to work a zip.

On skis they exhibit all the characteristics of a hit-and-run driver, and couldn't stop even if they wanted to. Their technique hasn't progressed beyond a 60 mph snow-plough. Unfortunately they are nearly always British.

The Freeloader

Usually ski journalists, these self-appointed epicureans rarely ski, not because they can't but because they prefer to remain in bars and restaurants and ventilate pompously on their 'coverage'.

Freeloaders are rarely distinguished by their appearance, but a sure giveaway is the loudness of their complaints when something doesn't meet with their approval (usually when they have to pay).

Instructors and Guides

Male ski-instructors are dangerous. Almost to a man they are over-sexed, amoral, utterly ruthless, vain, impatient, and completely irresistible to women. The lucky bastards.

Male ski-guides are even more deadly. Unlike instructors they are required to be polite and therefore create a false sense of security. They lure their clients into tricky situations, then deliberately humiliate male clients by having to rescue them. This impresses female clients, who then find them even more irresistible than instructors.

Female instructors wear expressions of extreme boredom brought about by years of exposure to small children on skis, and pigs-on-planks who should know better than to try to molest them. Female instructors are amongst the most dangerous women in the world to molest. If you try it they can effortlessly kill you and make it look like an accident.

The Pisteur/Ski Patrolman

Charged with the impossible task of keeping order on the slopes and clearing them of bodies after a day's skiing, pisteurs are either frustrated policemen or would-be instructors who didn't quite make the grade. Either way, they are generally angry about everything. Occasionally they are required to do something mundane like rope off a section of piste which makes them angrier than ever.

In America ski 'patrolmen' wear mirrored sunglasses and feel they should be allowed to shoot people. They make do with hiding in trees to catch people speeding. Then they clamp a flashing blue light to their hats and set off in hot pursuit.

The Artificier

Highest grade of pisteur – viz. those qualified to use explosives to 'aid' avalanches and blow up persistent offenders. It is not a good idea to smoke too near them, or do anything which might incur their displeasure.

The Ski-bum

Professional spongers who hang around ski resorts sleeping uninvited on chalet girls' floors, depleting the week's food and drink stock, latching on to groups of guests in the hope of a free drink, and, on the rare occasions they manage to crawl out of bed in time, spending most of their time on the mountain (courtesy of someone else's lift pass) clutching their heads and whining pitifully.

The First-timer

First-timers are to be deeply envied. No skier will ever again have as much fun falling over and laughing uncontrollably at everything. First-timers are made conspicuous by their verbal diarrhoea, permanent grins, and muddy backsides. It usually takes them about two to three days to become serious bluffers.

GLOSSARY

Aerials – Freestyle skiing discipline which show-offs perform to impress the opposite sex.

Abfahrt – German for 'descent' much in evidence on signs in Austria and Switzerland. Source of endless amusement to English-speaking children of all ages.

Apartment – Small cupboard in the French Alps. Useful for storing a pair of ski boots and not much else.

Bottleneck – Mayhem encountered in: a) a section of piste which is too narrow for ski-traffic; b) a permanent lift queue.

Bowl – Any treeless expanse of skiing terrain which looks like a bowl. 'Back' bowls are more in vogue than any other sort because they suggest that they are some distance from help. This is often the case.

Caught-an-edge – Instinctive explanation for falling over.

Caulfeild, **Vivien** – Seminal early British ski-writer: *How to Ski* (1910). Famous for spelling 'field' wrong.

Chalet-hotel – Hybrid form of accommodation which has all the disadvantages associated with hotels and none of the advantages associated with chalets (like unlimited free wine).

Couloir – French for corridor. A very steep, very narrow, very cool section of ski terrain.

Counter-rotation – Alarming physical phenomenon in which the upper body turns the opposite way from the lower body during a skiing manoeuvre.

DIN – Loud noise; the acronym for German standards

organisation which has a disproportionate influence on ski design.

Drag lift – Any ski-lift which drags skiers up a mountain in maximum discomfort.

Flapping – What a soft ski does at speed on hard snow. Also what the most irritating member of your party does all the time.

Foam injection – Excruciatingly painful means of providing ski-boots with a 'perfect' moulded fit. Don't believe it.

Gunbarrel – 'U'-shaped piste with high curving sides and a carpet of moguls. You'd be better off looking into the other sort.

Heli-skiing – An expensive form of ski-lift. Heli-skiers always hum *The Ride of the Valkyries* once airborne, much to the irritation of the pilot.

Hooking – Increasingly popular justification for falling over due to over-sharpened edges which 'hook' the snow.

Hot-dog – Freestyle skiing discipline which has something to do with moguls and nothing to do with sausages.

Inner skiing – Quaint theory about discovering skiing technique from within. Worth trying if all else fails.

Le fart – French for ski-wax which English-speakers find even more entertaining than the German for descent.

Linked – Term for connecting pistes by ski-lifts, or connecting your turns by not falling over.

Moonboot – Form of footwear, usually covered in

fake fur, which makes the wearer look like a Hobbit.

Motorway – Name given to wide, easy, cruising pistes much beloved by bluffers.

Piste map – Remarkable example of advanced origami.

Pschitt – Brand of soft fizzy drink in the Alps with a silent 'P'. Immensely popular with English-speaking children who demand it, loudly, all the time.

Rep – Someone to blame when there isn't any snow. Or to blame anyway.

Ski evolutif – French theory that all skiers are descended from apes. Apparently they graduated from short skis to long skis in evolutionary stages.

Snow-chains – Means of securing recalcitrant children in rear seats on ski-drive holidays. Also to wrap round tyres in icy conditions (chains, not children).

Transfer – Deliberately innocuous name given to interminable coach journey between airport and resort.

Warren Miller – American director of extreme ski movies able to persuade fit young men to hurl themselves off precipices and land in wheelchairs.

Wipe-out – Popular means of describing an inability to remain upright and still attached to one's skis.

Zdarsky, Mathias – The 'father' of Alpine skiing. He wrote *Lilienfelder Skilauf-Technik* (1896). Should be beside every ski-bluffer's bedside.

THE AUTHOR

Born in the Black Country in 1954, David Allsop's introduction to skiing was on a rudimentary mono-ski down the slopes of a slag heap in Quarry Bank. He spent the next 30-odd years scrupulously avoiding anything to do with sliding downhill.

Persuaded to go on a skiing trip to Cervinia in the mid 1980s, he instantly became the sort of fount of skiing knowledge that people fight to sit next to at dinner parties. Unaccountably, he finds invitations to dine have become somewhat more elusive.

After 20 trial careers in occupations as diverse as growing beansprouts and working as a barrister, he found his niche amidst the peaks and troughs of freelance journalism – adding ski-writing to his formidable portfolio of areas of professed expertise.

By dint of bluff and good luck he has managed to ski, at little cost to himself, in over 200 resorts – with a skiing style that was once described by a member of the Compagnie des Guides as 'comme une vache espagnole'* which he chooses to regard as a rare example of French irony.

He is married to another hopelessly addicted skier and lives in Blackheath, London (altitude 127 metres).

* 'Like a Spanish cow'.